The Art of
Fighting Without Fighting

Techniques in Personal Threat Evasion

Geoff Thompson

SUMMERSDALE

Summersdale Publishers Ltd
46 West Street
Chichester
West Sussex
PO19 1RP
United Kingdom

www.summersdale.com

Photographs by David W Monks
Member of the Master Photographer's Association
Snappy Snaps Portrait Studio
7 Cross Cheaping
Coventry
CV1 1HF

Printed and bound in Great Britain.

ISBN 1 84024 085 7

About the Author:

Geoff Thompson has written over 20 published books and is known world wide for his autobiographical books Watch My back, Bouncer and On The Door, about his nine years working as a night club doorman. He holds the rank of 5th Dan black belt in Japanese karate, 1st Dan in Judo and is also qualified to senior instructor level in various other forms of wrestling and martial arts. He has several scripts for stage, screen and TV in development with Destiny Films.

He has published several articles for GQ magazine, and has also been featured in FHM, Maxim, Arena, Front and Loaded magazines, and has been featured many times on mainstream TV.

Geoff is currently a contributing editor for Men's Fitness magazine and self defence columnist for Front.

Other books and videos by Geoff Thompson:

Watch My Back – A Bouncer's Story
Bouncer (sequel to *Watch My Back*)
On the Door – *Further Bouncer Adventures.*
The Pavement Arena
– *Adapting Combat Martial Arts to the Street*
Real Self-defence
Real Grappling
Real Punching
Real Kicking
Real Head, Knees & Elbows
Dead Or Alive – *Self-protection*
3 Second Fighter – The Sniper Option
Weight Training – For the Martial Artist
Animal Day – Pressure Testing the Martial Arts
Fear – The Friend of Exceptional People: techniques in controlling fear
Small Wars – How To Live A Stress Free Life
Blue Blood on the Mat by Athol Oakley, foreword by Geoff Thompson
Give Him To The Angels
– *The Story Of Harry Greb* by James R Fair

The Ground Fighting Series (books):
Vol. One   – Pins, the Bedrock
Vol. Two   – Escapes
Vol. Three   – Chokes and Strangles
Vol. Four   – Arm Bars and Joint Locks
Vol. Five   – Fighting From Your Back
Vol. Six   – Fighting From Neutral Knees

Videos:

Lessons with Geoff Thompson
Animal Day – Pressure Testing the Martial Arts
Animal Day Part Two   – The Fights
Three Second Fighter   – The Sniper Option
Throws and Take-Downs Vols. 1-6
Real Punching Vols. 1-3
The Fence

The Ground Fighting Series (videos):

Vol. One   – Pins, the Bedrock
Vol. Two   – Escapes
Vol. Three   – Chokes and Strangles
Vol. Four   – Arm Bars and Joint Locks
Vol. Five   – Fighting From Your Back
Vol. Six   – Fighting From Neutral Knees

Advanced Ground Fighting Vols. 1-3

Pavement Arena Part 1
Pavement Arena Part 2
        – The Protection Pyramid
Pavement Arena Part 3
        – Grappling, The Last Resort
Pavement Arena Part 4
        – Fit To Fight

Contents:

Introduction

There was once a very famous Aikido player in Japan who spent his whole life studying Usheba's legendary art. Although he had dedicated his whole existence to this beautiful art he had never actually had occasion to test it in a real life situation against a determined attacker, someone intent on hurting him. Being a moralistic kind of person he realised that it would be very bad karma to actually go out and pick a fight just to test his art so he was forced to wait until a suitable occasion presented itself. Naively, he longed for the day when he was attacked so that he could prove to himself that Aikido was powerful outside of the controlled walls of the dojo.

The more he trained, the more his obsession for validation grew until one day, travelling home from work on a local commuter train, a potential situation did present itself – an overtly drunk and aggressive man boarded his train and almost immediately started verbally abusing the other passengers.

'This is it,' the Aikido man thought to himself, 'this is my chance to test my art.'

He sat waiting for the abusive passenger to reach him. It was inevitable that he would: he was making his way down the carriage abusing everyone in his path. The drunk got closer and closer to the Aikido man, and the closer he got the louder and more aggressive he became. Most of the other passengers recoiled in fear of being attacked by the drunk. However, the Aikido man couldn't wait for his turn, so that he could prove to himself and everyone else, the effectiveness of his art. The drunk got closer and louder. The Aikido man made ready for the seemingly inevitable assault – he readied himself for a bloody encounter.

As the drunk was almost upon him he prepared to demonstrate his art in the ultimate arena, but before he could rise from his seat the passenger in front of him stood up and engaged the drunk jovially. 'Hey man, what's up with you? I bet you've been drinking in the bar all day, haven't you? You look like a man with problems. Here, come and sit down with me, there's no need to be abusive. No one on this train wants to fight with you.'

The Aikido man watched in awe as the passenger skilfully talked the drunken man down from his rage. Within minutes the drunk was pouring his heart out to the passenger about how his life had taken a downward turn and how he had fallen on hard times. It wasn't long before the drunk had tears streaming down his face. The Aikido man, somewhat ashamed thought to himself 'That's Aikido!'. He realised in that instant that the passenger with a comforting arm around the sobbing drunk was demonstrating Aikido, and all martial art, in it highest form.

Why have I written this book? Why have I written a book about the art of fighting without fighting when my claim to fame is probably the fact that I have been in over 300 street fights, where I used a physical response to neutralise my enemy. Why write a book about avoidance when it is obviously so simple to finish a fight with the use of a physical attack? Indeed why write it when my whole reputation as a realist, as a martial arts cross trainer, as a blood and snot mat man may be risked by the endeavour? The reason is simple: violence is not the answer! It may solve some of the problems in the short term but it will create a lot more in the long term. I know – I've been there. I was, as they say, 'that soldier'.

It took me nine years of constant violence and many more of soul-searching to realise this truth and because so much has happened to me in my post-'door' years, my attitude and opinion has changed. At my most brutal I justified violence, to myself, to those I taught and to those I spoke to. I was even prepared to use verbal violence to substantiate my views. That was how lost I was. But I'm not at all ashamed of that, my views may have been distorted then but I did genuinely believe them. I was never a bad person, it's just that my beliefs were governed by my limited knowledge, which left me somewhat Neanderthal.

As my knowledge has grown so has my intellect and confidence, this has allowed me a new belief – a belief that will keep changing as long I grow. I can see it all now. I can see where I fit into the scheme of things. I can see the futility of violence and the pain of violent people. I can see that fighting on the pavement arena is war in microcosm and that wars destroy worlds. I know now that violence is not the answer, in the short term or the long

term. There has to be another solution. At this moment in time I cannot tell you what that solution is, only that knocking a guy unconscious and doing a 56 move kata on his head is not it. Not if we are ever going to survive as a species and learn to live in peace with one another. I spend my time now trying to avoid violence and trying to develop alternatives to taking an opponent off the planet with a practised right cross. Some of the stuff is good too, it works, it will at least help keep some of the antagonists at bay until we can find a better alternative.

But, I hear you cry, what about those who won't let you avoid, escape, dissuade, loophole, posture, the ones that not only take you to the doorway of violence but want to kick it open and enter the arena and no amount of talk or negotiation is going to stop them. What are we to do with or to them? Well, this is where my 'non-violence' theorem becomes a little contradictory, because if we are forced into a physical response and if we do not fight back, our species is as good as dead.

I, like most, have a family to protect and I will protect by whatever means fair or foul. Because I am trying to become a better person, and because I am desperately trying to lose violence from my life, I have been struggling with the fact that, occasionally when it is unavoidable, I may still have to employ violence, if only to keep the peace. I am constantly struggling with the fact that this still feels wrong to me, but my, our, survival is at stake. When I was in America last year (1997) I was teaching with Benny 'the jet' Urquidiz and I asked him whether he thought, given the fact that we were both trying to be Christian people, you could ever justify the use of violence. He told me that he believed violence was wrong, but if someone left you no other option other than to hit him, then it was their karma, it was meant to be. He said that he felt they were sent by God to be taught a lesson and he would give that lesson as gently as possible.

Some people need a poke in the eye to show them the right direction, others simply need pointing in the right direction. It is a question of having the wisdom to know when to point and when to poke. To some in society violence is a language, a way of communication – a very primitive language – but a means of discourse nonetheless. If you don't speak to them in their own tongue, then they will not understand you. This is where the contention begins.

So, we have a contradiction in play here: violence is wrong but sometimes we have to employ it. I know that the uninitiated are already up in arms, probably scribbling away discontent to the letters page as we speak. I truly understand how they feel, because I feel the same way, but I fear that they will never be convinced by words, and their experience of life is often not broad enough to give them another perspective. Their truth for a completely violence-free world is as limited by their finite perspective, as mine was as a nightclub doorman. I needed to experience the hope of non-violence to appreciate its potential. They probably need to experience violence to appreciate its necessity as an antidote in a world where the species is lowly evolved.

I have a varied background in these matters. I have experienced violence, pre-bouncer, as a scared young man who could only suffer in silence. I have also experienced violence as man who could confidently counter it with greater violence and I now experience a violent world as a man who can confidently employ violence but who chooses not to because I feel it is not the answer. Most people's opinions are born from experiencing only one of these perspectives.

As a nightclub doorman I was often faced by violence that terrified me, woundings that revolted me and conduct that chilled me to the bone. However, what really sickened me – even more than the congealed blood and smashed teeth of an adversary – was the absolute hypocrisy of this fickle society. Facing adversity did show me the beauty of amity but it took time, many savage confrontations and much self-education, before I could drag myself kicking and screaming into a better existence. Unfortunately, even then I could not find a preferable solution to the threat of immediate attack than that of counter-attack. I am aware that the state might call my actions criminal, but how do they rationalise their own acts of violence? Perhaps by calling them law? I teach many strategies to evade attack; avoidance, escape, verbal dissuasion, loopholing and posturing. But what do you do when all of these techniques have been exhausted and you are still facing an adversary that wants to step outside the law and attack you? You are left with a choice, either become the hammer or the anvil – hurt or be hurt, kill or be killed. Does that sound brutal? Are these the words of an uneducated nightclub thug? How would you deal with the situation? How would your peers deal with it? Those in government? Those with power?

Without wishing to go into politics and the rights and wrongs of what is going on in the world, I will offer an example of how they, the leaders of the free world, the highbrow of humanity, deal with potentially violent situations that will not go away. The world recently found itself in a very threatening situation with a foreign leader, a threat that could potentially destroy the world and effect many other planets in our solar system. The United Nations, the immune system of the world, tried to avoid a violent confrontation by mediation. The UN tried to escape a violent situation with compromise, they 'loopholed' by trying to offer 'the threat' honourable alternatives to war, they 'postured' by threatening war, (even flying bomber planes over his country in a threatening manner). They absolutely exhausted mediation. When it all failed, what did the United Nation do, what did they consider justifiable, though unfortunate, what did they greatest minds in the free world agree upon when all their avoidance techniques did not work? WAR! War was what they agreed upon! War: the greatest expression of violence known to man, where thousands of men, women and children are killed and maimed. The UN told this leader in no uncertain terms that they were prepared to talk to him, that they wanted to avoid war, that they wanted to find an alternative to bloodshed but the bottom line was, if he did not comply, they would kill him and his people!'

The immune system recognises cancerous cells, it knows that one cancerous cell can destroy the whole body if it is not killed, so it sends out killer T-cells to assassinate the threatening cell. Ugly, but necessary if you want the body, and the species to survive.

As for me working with violence? Physically the toll was bearable, if not a little hideous. My nose, broken in three places (I'll never go to those places again!) stab scars in my head, broken knuckles and fingers and a cauliflower ear that could win a horticultural ribbon. But some of my friends were not so lucky: three lost their lives, a couple their marbles and yet another lost the sight in one eye to a glass-wielding psychopath.

Psychologically however my wounds were less superfluous. Overexposure to the brutality of people left me temporarily paranoid, cynical and often very violent. I could see only physical solutions to life's many disputes. Punching an adversary unconscious after an argument was, to me, as perfunctory as a mint after dinner. It was never gratuitous, I hated fighting, it was survival, and that was all. In my world violence was a plumber's wrench – no more than that. This behaviour was acceptable, even expectable but in civvy street, me and my kind were brandished Neanderthal. So when I finally transcended 'the door' there was a time of readjustment, of trying to locate my place in a capricious society where doormen were seen as vogue in times of trouble and vague in times of peace.

I was frequently informed by those who had not met violence down a dark alley (and it's too easy to say when you haven't 'been there'), that violence was not the answer – a view voiced so often these days that it has almost become a fashion accessory. Not an easy standard to apply though when faced by a savage adversary intent on flattening the world with your head. How many would not employ even the vilest instrument to protect a loved one? For instance the young lady who nearly burst my ear drum out side a Coventry nightclub would never have believed herself capable of violent assault, yet when her beloved was attacked her principles disappeared quicker than a gambler's rent money. 'Violence is not the answer!' She yelled at me indignantly. Granted I had just 'sparked' her irate boyfriend with a practised right cross. He had tried to marry my face with the speared edges of a broken beer glass – I felt compelled to stop him the only way I knew how.

'No?' I replied with mock surprise. 'Well, tell your boyfriend that when he wakes up.'

My reply angered her so much that her face contorted into a domino of hate. She proceeded to remove a stiletto heel from her elegant foot, hoist the makeshift weapon above her head like an executioner's axe and attempt to separate me from my mortality. She was about to employ violence to accentuate her point that it was 'not the answer'.

It would seem that hypocrisy in our society knows no bounds. Ironically my own life as a bouncer began due to my own innate fear of violence. I donned the required 'tux' in the hope that confronting my fears might nurture a greater understanding of my own sympathetic nervous system, one that seemed in a permanent state of alert, maybe even descry a little desensitisation. It was to be an eventful, if not bloody journey that lasted nine years. En route I discovered that truths that can only usually be found in the middle of stormy oceans or at the top of craggy mountains. Nothing comes free of course, and there is a consequence to every action that we take; if you pick up one end of the stick you also pick up the other. Enlightenment came at great expense. My innocence was clubbed like a beached seal, my marriage ended in bitter divorce and my faith in human nature took a near near-fatal slash to the jugular.

So, I realise that until the species we call humankind evolves, there will always be a need for violence (unfortunately, I have no doubt about this in my mind) to protect the good majority and the world, from the bad minority and the indifferent from themselves. This doesn't make violence right, rather it is a necessary evil – sometimes you have to lose a finger to save a hand. This does not mean that everyone has to partake in violence, or even agree on its necessity, on a large scale to protect this world from those who would inadvertently destroy it. Many people make the mistake of thinking that a solution must be palatable to be correct – this couldn't be farther from the truth. Violence to prevent greater violence will never be more than a hideous expression of physical domination, but it may save mankind until its metamorphosis into a spiritual domain.

Therefore, not everyone has to 'get their hands dirty'. There will always be a select few, like the killer T-cells in the body, that roam the bloodstream protecting the body from the intrusion of viral cells, who are chosen to do the dirty work in the name of those who won't or can't. The immune system protects the body this way, and even God in his infinite wisdom had warring angels in Heaven to fight evil. Returning to my original questions: why did I write this book, why do I teach avoidance techniques? Because violence is wrong and one of the best remedies is to attack proactively so that we can avoid, escape, dissuade, loophole or posture to avoid physical confrontation and prevent violence from becoming manifest. I believe that a part of the evolution of our species is to rid the world of violence, so I would like to explore as many ways of avoiding fighting as I can. If all we know is 'a punch on the nose', then, when the shit hits the fan and contention is on the menu, we will have no other choice but to employ a punch on the nose. If, however, we have several other alternatives to choose from, and we can become expert in using these alternatives, then we can strategically evade the use of force, and still ensure victory most of the time.

As with all my concepts, this book is pieced together from empirical study in the field. None of it is theory, I have made it all work on many occasions against fearsome opponents who wanted to part me from my mortality, or from my good looks at the very least!

When I started in the martial arts my 'ippon', my knock out, my tap-out was to beat my opponents with the use of physical force. My objectives have now changed. Now if I have to hit some one to win the day I feel that no one has won. So my ippon now is to beat someone using guile as opposed to force. My hope is that this book will encourage the same in you.

Chapter One

Avoidance

Avoidance is the very first in a long list of tactical manoeuvres aimed at 'not being there' when an attack is taking place. And it really is very simple, even obvious, but I find it is the 'simple' and 'obvious' stuff that usually gets overlooked and lands people in an affray that should never have occurred. These tactics are not to be read and stored, rather they are to be read and practised over and over again until they are natural, everyday habits, like getting into the car and putting on your seat-belt, (something that once had to be forced is now a habit). In fact, I bet if you tried driving without a seat belt it would feel awkward after wearing one for so long. Avoidance is being aware, understanding the enemy, understanding yourself and understanding your environment. If you are training in a martial art, then avoidance is understanding that art and whether it will stand up to the threat of a real encounter. More than anything, avoidance is having enough control over yourself, your ego, your pride, peer pressure, morality etc. to stop these negative emotions

from dragging you into a situation that could otherwise be avoided.

Many people find themselves fighting because they are worried about what others might think if they run away. If you are very confident in yourself and you know your capabilities you will have no problem walking away, or simply not being there in the first place. Insecure people, those that are not sure of themselves or their art, will be fighting all day long because they lack the strength of character to go against popular opinion. This is often the case with martial artists (no offence intended), especially high graded ones. They are frequently on such a high pedestal (placed there by themselves, or by their own pupils) that they drag themselves into fights that could/should be avoided, because they are worried about letting their students down in some way. This is often their own fault because they have taught a 'corporal' system that only addresses the physical response – the ultimate accolade being a KO when attacked by an assailant.

I understand this; it is a syndrome that I too went through as a young instructor. As a man that has 'been there', my ideals have changed and whilst the physical response is, obviously, still on my training curriculum, it is no longer my main artillery, neither is the physical ippon (KO) my main aim. Rather my goal is to defeat an opponent without becoming physical.

In theory, I am aware that this aim is simple and straightforward, in reality in a confrontational society such as ours it is not so easy – a tremendous amount of self-control and confidence is needed to make this lofty goal an actuality. This is predominantly why I make my personal system of combat such a difficult one: to develop this confidence and control. This is also the reason why our motto is the latin 'Per Ardua Et Astra' (through hardship to the stars), and why such people as the American Dog brothers work with the motto 'higher consciousness through harder contact'.

Jeff Cooper, legendary American close combat and shooting instructor (known on the circuit as this generation's closest thing to Wyatt Earp), was once asked how you would know if your art was effective for street defence or self-protection. His reply was simple: when you are worried about hurting, perhaps killing another human being because your technique is so potent, then you know your art is real.

Do you feel that way, or are you still worrying/wondering whether your art will in fact even work in that arena? If your feelings fall into the latter category it is worth injecting a little more pressure in your training and putting your system to the test in the controlled arena, by taking it as close to the real thing (under supervision) as possible. This can also mean watching extreme fighting tapes to see how the innovators are doing it.

The key phrase for avoidance in contemporary self-protection is 'Target Hardening'. By making yourself a hard target, you lessen your chances of being chosen as a potential victim. I once interviewed a group of burglars, I asked them for their prime requisite when selecting a house to rob. This was their response:

'We always look for properties that are not protected.' The house that sported an alarm box, dog pictures in the window, window locks etc. were very often by-passed by the average robber.

The Art of Fighting Without Fighting

'Why bother bursting your balls on a dwelling with all that protection when there are rakes of houses around the corner with **ck all, just asking to be robbed. These people kill us. They ****ing gripe about having their houses robbed yet they leave us an invite at the door. They just make it easy for us.'

Many burglars rob the same house three or more times, because the owners do nothing to stop them. Self-protection works in a similar vein. If you make yourself a hard target by following the rules of awareness, you too will by by-passed for an 'easier target'. If you don't you will be chosen again and again.

The contemporary enemy likes to work via dialogue and deception. An understanding the enemy and his rituals is imperative, if you are ever going to avoid his onslaught (see Dead Or Alive). So many people these days say that they train for self-defence – yet they know nothing about the enemy that they are training to fight or the environment that they are planning to fight in – then they wonder why they get their heads kicked in when a situation goes 'live'. Many such people ask me, 'Where did I go wrong?' I have a profound love for people, for my species, and I don't want to see innocent people getting battered when they could so easily, with a little information, have avoided a physical scenario. Here are a few of the things that I have picked up on my travels about the modern enemy. Note: It is important here to stress one point, fighting in the street is rarely match fighting. Most affrays of the modern era are 'three second fights': attacks preceded by dialogue that is used as a leading technique to create a window of entry for a devastating physical attack, that usually takes the victim out of the game before he even knows that he is in it.

Match fighting, as honourable as it is, is an arena that died with my fathers' generation. If you do find yourself in a match fight scenario I will bet my trousers that the fight will go to ground within seconds (most fighters are grossly ill prepared for ground fighting). If the three second fight goes more that the usual three, then in all likelihood this too will end up in a match fight that will end on the floor. If you can ground fight, great, you can tear the guy a new arse. If you can't you should expect at the very least an elongated fight, perhaps even a brutal loss. If the guy is not on his own and you are facing two or more opponents then you can expect to be hospitalised, even killed. Two of my friends were stabbed by women when they were ground fighting with men.

Ambush fighting is what you get nine times out of ten if you are not switched on, or coded up, as they say (see colour codes). An ambush fight is when the first you know of the fight is a physical attack. If the guy who attacks you is worth his salt as a street fighter then that first blow is likely to be the last in the fight and you should get used to hospital food because that's what you will be getting. If you are switched on to the enemy and the environment yourself, then you will avoid nearly all of the potential attacks. Those that are unavoidable, you will be able to control, those beyond your control you will be able to defend against.

The four D's are often used by attackers, especially muggers and rapists. 'Dialogue' is the priming tool, the leading technique used by many attackers. The attacker does not lead or open with a jab or a lead leg roundhouse, he leads with dialogue, and is often either aggressive or very deceptive. If you do not understand this then you will be suckered into the first attack. Dialogue, and often appearance, is used to 'deceive' the victim before attack. Nearly every attack I have ever documented that was not a blind side, ambush attack (the ones that happen when you do not use awareness) always arose through deception – the attacker using this as a window of entry. The rule of thumb with the unsolicited attacker is if his lips move he's lying. If anyone approaches, it is imperative that you employ a protective fence immediately (see 'fence' later). Most attacks are launched under the guise of deception, for the street fighter 'that's the art', you might moan that it is dishonourable, a Judas attack, unfair etc. but the bottom line will still be the same – he won and you lost. The fact that you might think it dishonourable demonstrates your lack of understanding of the modern enemy. There is no honour in war, and this is war in microcosm.

'Distraction' is a part of deception and usually comes through dialogue. The attacker may ask his victim a question and then initiate attack when the brain is engaged. The distraction, or brain engagement, also switches off any in-built spontaneous, physical response the victim may have. A man with twenty years of physical training in a fighting art under his belt can be stripped of his ability by this simple ploy. I have witnessed many trained fighters, who are monsters in the controlled arena, get beaten by a guy with only an ounce of their physical ability. How? They were distracted before the attack. Rob, a hardened street fighter and nightclub doorman always told his potential attackers that he didn't want to fight before he attacked them. Invariably they would come around from their unconscious stupor, after Rob had knocked them unconscious, some seconds later muttering 'I' m sure he said he didn't want to fight!'

If the distraction is submissive; 'I don't want any trouble, can we talk about it?' This will take your assailant from Code Red (when a person is ready for 'fight' or 'flight') to Code White (a state of non-awareness). The submissiveness will intimate that the danger is over and he'll go into a state of relief. Brain engagement, via disarming/distracting dialogue gives the victim a 'blind second'. This is when the assailant strikes. The distraction technique is also used by the experienced attacker to take down any protective fences that may have been constructed by the victim. This final product of expert priming is your destruction. Few victims survive the first physical blow and most are 'out of the game', before they even realise that they are in it, because many street attackers are pro's with one or two physical techniques that have been tried, tested and perfected on numerous, previous victims.

Even trained martial artists get fooled by the four D's, because they do not appear on their training curriculum. Therefore, they do not understand the enemy that they are facing and so also fail to grasp – and therefore translate – 'street speak', the mass deception often causing disorientation. The attacker uses the former and latter to prime a victim that is only trained in 'physical response'. As I have already stated, deceptive dialogue is the professional attacker's leading technique. Understanding this will allow you greater awareness, it will keep you 'switched on'. Being switched on to all of the forgoing is the better part of 'Target Hardening'.

If and when a situation does become 'live', it is again imperative that you understand yourself and what will happen to your body in its preparation for fight or flight. You will usually experience a huge injection of adrenaline (and other stress hormones) into the system (adrenal dump). Adrenaline can add speed, strength and anaesthesia to response but, unfortunately, because very few people have regular exposure to the adrenal syndrome their reasoning process often mistakes it for fear. Consequently many people 'freeze' under its influence. Therefore a profound understanding of fear needs to be sought. If you can' t control the person on the inside then it is safe to say that you cannot control the person on the out side (the attacker).

Jeff Cooper devised a colour coding system to help recognise, evaluate and subsequently avoid potential threat. The codes are a yardstick designed to measure rising threat and, if adhered to, make most situations become avoidable. Cooper designed the codes of awareness to allow people a 360 degree environmental awareness. What I would like to add to this, with respect to the great man, is also awareness of attack ritual, physical reality and of bodily reactions to confrontation – after all awareness is a complex thing.

Code White is known as 'switched off', unaware of environment, inhabitants and their ritual of attack. Code White is the victim state that all attackers look for. They usually don't have to look far because most people are completely switched off most of the time.

Code Yellow is threat awareness. Known as 'switched on', this state of perception allows 360 degree peripheral awareness of environmental vulnerability. For example the awareness of secluded doorways, entries etc. and the psychological dangers of untested physical artillery (self-defence techniques that have not been pressure tested) adrenal dump, attackers rituals etc. Initially, Code Yellow is similar to commentary driving, where you talk through and describe, as you drive, everything you can see around you. Similarly, as you walk, run a subconscious commentary of everything that is happening in your locale, ultimately, with practice, managing the same without verbalising the commentary. Code Yellow is the state of mind which everyone adopts whilst crossing a busy road. It is not a state of paranoia, rather a state of heightened observance.

Code Orange represents rising threat, allowing evaluation if circumstances in your locale deteriorate. For instance, you may, as you walk, notice a couple of suspicious-looking men over the road from you. If they begin to cross in your direction with menacing intent, and you feel there is a possible threat, Code Orange will allow assessment and evaluation of the situation.

Code Red is the final stage. You have evaluated the situation in Code Orange. If there is a threat, prepare to fight or run. Never stand and fight if there is a possibility of flight. If no threat presents itself, drop back to Orange and Yellow. Never lose your awareness and drop to White – many people have been beaten in real situations because they have lost their zanshin (awareness). Stay switched on.

Of course this whole system works on the premise that you are in Code Yellow in the first place. You cannot go into an evaluation state on a situation that you have not noticed developing, equally you cannot prepare for fight or flight if you have not seen and evaluated the same. In this case the first you are likely to know of the situation is when it is too late. The same applies with the following rules, if you are 'switched off' none of them are likely to apply, you need to be in Code Yellow (switched on) to make any use of them at all. So in all cases, 'Code Up'.

Avoid the places that are trouble spots. Don't drink in shit holes or eat in late night Indian restaurants that attract those who have just left (or have been kicked out of) a nightclub. Try and avoid frequenting areas that are rough, and if you have to, make sure that you are totally switched on at all times.

I have no problem with my ego, I won't be drawn into a road rage incident because some lemon stole the piece of road in front of me, or cut me up, or sped past me etc. My mum always told me (it must be true because mums don't lie) that there is no rush to the graveyard. Therefore, if the spanner in front wants my space, I'm quite happy to let him

If the spanner in front wants my space – he can have it.

have it; if he is flashing me to let him past, I'll let him past; if he beeps me or gives me the finger then I'll let it go. I already know where these situations are going to take me and I don't want to go there. I've been there before and believe me there are no winners. Incidents like this can change the course of your life if you let them. You kill someone, inadvertently in a road rage incident then you might as well stick your head between your legs and kiss your arse goodbye. And the little son or daughter that you have at home waiting for you, the beautiful wife that dotes on you, you can kiss them goodbye for 10-15 years as well.

One of my friends was driving home from a restaurant one night with his mate and their girlfriends. Quite legitimately they overtook a car on a quiet country road. The guy in the other car took offence to this and, pretended to swerve into my friend. I'm pretty sure that he only did it to scare my mate, nevertheless he thought that the guy was actually going to hit his car. He reacted by turning sharply to the right to avoid what he thought was going to be a collision and smashed his car up the bank. His beautiful girlfriend was thrown from the car and killed instantly. The other female passenger was thrown out of the other window and suffered terrible injuries, not least of which was total blindness in one eye. Both the male passengers were also badly injured. All of this happened because a driver took offence at someone overtaking him. When Karen died in that car crash a small part of many people, myself included, died with her. The man in the offending car will have to live with the death of Karen for the rest of his life.

Another friend of mine has just committed a crime of passion – one that could have been ignored if it wasn't for his very large ego – that will place him in jail for at least 10 years. By the time he is released, if the experience doesn't kill him, his schoolgirl daughter will probably be a married woman with kids of her own. His wife will have probably moved on and married someone else, very few wait around. He has gone in to jail in his late thirties, the prime of his life, when he is released he will be approaching fifty. His business, to which he devoted himself, has already gone down the drain.

Think about it for a single second, not being able to be with your wife and kids for ten years, not being able to walk in the park; go for a pizza; drink a pint; cuddle up to your wife in her silk nightie. Doesn't the very thought frighten the shit out of you? It frightens me.

If I get into a fight and have to hurt someone, I want the reason to be a better one than protecting a space by the bar, or a piece of tarmac on a country road. I want to be lying in my bed thinking to myself, 'I had no other option open to me but to fight'. There is a heavy toll to pay for participating in a fight and, if you are morally in the wrong, the bill that drops through the door can be very exacting. Once again, we return to the fact that your system should be real, if it is, and you pressure test what you have, then the confidence it brings will be enough to enable you to walk away – it will make you strong enough to over ride peer pressure and ego.

A pivotal part of understanding the enemy is realising that he probably doesn't understand himself very well. When he gives you the finger in the car, or stares at you aggressively across a busy bar it's not personal, unless of course you make it so. You are a manifestation of whatever it is in his life that makes him angry: his dominant wife; his bullying boss; his car that keeps breaking down or his adolescent children. You become a displacement figure for the things in life that cause him stress. It's only because we take these incidents personally that we find ourselves being drawn into contentious situations. If you think about it, that's probably why you find yourself getting angry with people (especially those closest to you), over little or nothing – you are also displacing your unutilised aggression.

The combination of our confrontational society and increasing amounts of neurological stressors means that we are bound to develop pent-up aggression. Stores of stress hormones sit waiting to be released by our behaviour, awaiting the right trigger to let them go off with a bang. That trigger might be a minor traffic incident, it may be some lemon staring at you across the bar, or something as simple as one of your children spilling juice on the carpet. Once triggered, the pent-up aggression explodes in an uncontrolled manner that can change the course of your life, for the worse, forever.

Understanding the enemy means comprehending that, 'it's not personal' and that, if a situation becomes physical there are no winners. Once you understand the psyche of the person or people that you are dealing with, you will probably understand them better than they understand themselves. In an instant you will be able to see and understand the run of their whole life and that it, like so many, is on a downward spiral to oblivion. Don't you find that very sad? Doesn't it make you feel a little compassion for these people? Not only do they not understand where they are going wrong, they will probably never understand and their whole life will unravel in the same unfortunate way. Don't take it personally, let it go, let them off! Their lives are already shit without you making it worse.

The Art of Fighting Without Fighting

I know what you will be saying, and I know what you mean. Just because it isn't personal doesn't mean that these people are not dangerous. Off course they are all potential killers, but usually only if you engage them and play the game that they want to play. The majority of the time these situations are benign until we counter their initial aggression, either because of our ego, some misdirected need to cleanse the world of bad people or the fact that we are reacting to the situation in a displaced manner ourselves. Imagine two guys, lets call them Joe and Pete, beating the crap out of each other over a minor a traffic incident. But they are not really fighting with each other. Pete is really battering his bullying boss and Joe is really battering his domineering wife. When they end up in court together neither will really be sure why they were fighting in the first place.

I consider my art to be hugely effective, I have pressure tested it to the full. I have worked my art on numerous occasions in real situations, so I can look at these minor altercations and let them go, knowing that I am letting the other guy off. It doesn't matter to me that he might think he has put one over on me, backed me down or that I have bottled it. I don't care what he thinks, or anyone else for that matter. I know the truth, I know that if forced I would have hurt that person very badly.

If displacement is in your face and you can' t walk away, if your can' t avoid, escape, dissuade, posture, loophole etc., then you may be forced to exercise your right to self-defence. Your karma will then be good and you will only be doing what you have to do. Perhaps as Benny 'the jet' Urquidiz suggested to me last year, they were sent by God for a lesson. Whatever the reason, you know that justification was your ally and that's enough.

Chapter Two

Escape

We all make mistakes, even monkeys fall out of trees, so there will be occasions when the option of avoidance will be lost and escape becomes the next option. In theory you would think that escape would be easy, it usually entails simply walking away, on occasions even running away. Not so! People of this generation are seen as cowards if the do not stand and face their problems 'like a man'. Ironically they are also seen as thugs if they stand and have a bloody fight to settle their differences. The law is quick to lock you up should you hurt someone too badly, even if it is in self-defence. This is why I call the law the second enemy. There is often only one thing standing between those that have a fight and those that run away – ego. This controlling muscle has had much exercise in this capricious society and is the curse of the 20th century. More fights and contentions are caused by the ego than any other single factor. This comes back to what I said earlier, correct training and combative hardship corrodes the control of the ego and puts you back in charge. You will no longer be dragged around the yard by your ego, you will have the confidence to walk away.

Escape is often a lot easier than one may think and doesn't always involve elaborate planning or strategy, just pure common sense.

The Art of Fighting Without Fighting

I have a friend in the south, a 6th Dan in karate, who rang me up to ask me to help him out with a dilemma. He regularly visited a local pub and every time he did there was a particular chap in there who stared him out in a challenging manner. You know the type, knuckles dragging along the floor, IQ of a plant.

'What should I do?' he asked.

'Drink somewhere else where the clientele are a little more intelligent,' I replied.

It really is that simple. If a pub is so rough that strangers want to stare at me for no other reason than they don't like the look of my face, then I do not want to drink there. Especially when you consider that most areas have hundreds of public houses to choose from. You might argue that you have every right to drink in that place and are not prepared to drink somewhere else, and that would be your right. But I come back to my original point, why would you want to defend a spot by a bar in a shit hole as contentious as that? Drink somewhere else. If I enter a bar and buy a drink for £2 and I start getting aggressive stares from some Neanderthal at the other end of the bar, I'll leave the drink and go somewhere else. For the sake of £2 I have saved myself a hell of a lot of trouble. I look at the worst case scenario. I know that if I stay where I am the lemon is going to approach me at some point in the night and a fight is going to ensue. Because my whole life is training, the chances are I am going to hurt the fellow very badly – probably hospitalise him. He goes to the hospital, I go to the police station where they charge me with a Section 18 wounding with intent. Because I train, the prosecuting council is going to make me out to be a superman and a jury of 12 are going to convict me for 5 years. Is a space by the bar in a shit hole of a pub really worth it? I don't think so.

Escape can mean as little as swallowing your pride or controlling your ego, taking your lady by the arm and moving to a place where your company is appreciated. If you are like me, have a little drink at home or go to a nice restaurant thus avoiding the potential all together and stopping you having to look over your shoulder every five minutes to see who is staring at you. If you find this difficult, if for some reason you are stuck in a particular place for the evening and a guy gives you the evil eye, lift your hand up and give the fellow a polite wave. The chances are that he will think that he knows you from somewhere and feel embarrassed that he has stared, he might even wave back. Once you have made the wave do not hold eye contact, this is often seen as a subliminal challenge.

If you were to bump into someone and they get a little aggressive make an apology – say you're sorry for bumping into them. Say it firmly, but politely, so that they can feel your confidence. If they pursue it place a fence between you and them and back away. Tell them that you don't want trouble. If they pursue it any further then you may have to get physical, perhaps with posturing (later chapter) or even an attack. If you do have to attack then make it pre-emptive. Blocking and countering like they do in the films doesn't work so don't bother trying.

An incident occurred recently when I was at the bar of a private party where I had no other option open to me than to stay. I went to the bar with Sharon and an ugly fellow stood by the bar started staring at me. I tried to be polite because I sensed that he wanted trouble.

'How you doing mate?' I asked very nicely.

'You a bodyguard?' he replied aggressively. We were at a private party for a large security company who hired static security men and bodyguards.

'Actually I'm not,' I replied honestly.

'Liar!' came the very rude response.

I nearly lost the plot at this point because the guy was overtly aggressive and it was obvious that he was looking for a fight. I lined him up to knock him out and remembered where I was and that I was trying to practice avoiding fights, I'd been in over three hundred and had seen enough bloodshed for ten lifetimes. I was very firm, slightly annoyed.

'No I'm not a liar, I am not a bodyguard.'

'What are you then?' Still aggressive.

'I'm a guest'.

'Fucking bodyguards, all a load of wankers!'

I turned away from him and got my drinks.

'Listen, forget it. I was just trying to be nice to you.'

As I walked away I heard him sneer, 'Fucking bodyguards, all a bunch of wankers'. Sharon patted me on the back and said, 'Well done'. She knew that two years earlier the guy would have been knocked unconscious, along with anyone else that stood in to defend him. But now I was practising a different art. For those that might be interested he tried the same thing on with my friend Griff, who was actually an international bodyguard. Griff smashed his nose into the toilet urinals – he wasn't as patient as I was.

It is often a lot easier to avoid a fight if you have an understanding of the attack ritual. As we said earlier: understand the enemy or you are fighting in the dark. If you know why, where and how an attack is likely to happen, it stands to reason that the acquired knowledge will help you to avoid such situations, or prepare for them.

There are, of course, lots of different types of attackers and attacks. Some choose to rob, some choose to rape, whilst others instigate gratuitous violence for no other profit than malice. Some assailants are cold-blooded in that they meticulously plan their attacks before they set about executing them. Many are opportunists who will only commit an offence if a 'safe' situation arises in their everyday lives. Men, women and children are being attacked indiscriminately, even in highly populated areas, where the frightened and seemingly unsympathetic general public hide under the veil of, 'It's nothing to do with me', or 'I don't want to get involved.' However when you have a judicial system that seems more in favour of the attacker than the victim this reticence is often understandable.

Generally the attacker of today is a cowardly person who either fights from the podium of alcohol/drugs or attacks from behind, possibly with the crutch of a weapon or an accomplice, or both. Excepting possibly the rapist, who often works on the basis that he believes himself physically superior to his victim, most attackers work with the aid of one or more accomplices. As formerly mentioned they are looking for VICTIMS, those that are in Code White or are detached from the herd. If you practice target hardening, these people – due to their proverbial 'yellow' streaks – will not cross your path. If they do and you fight back ferociously with well-aimed economical attacks, they will often abort, though I have to reiterate a physical response is the inferior tactic. If you do decide to employ physical techniques, make sure that you know your way around the fighting arena or you may just add anger to the attacker's artillery by daring to strike him. If you strike, you need to know that it will inflict damage enough for you to effect an escape.

Most attacks are preceded by stalking and dialogue entrapments. The 3 second fight is not commonly known or talked about, but most attackers use dialogue as their leading technique. I find that many instructors of self-defence are so concerned about the physical 'tricks' that they forget about those vital seconds leading up to assault. It is those that handle pre-fight most effectively that tend to be victorious when a situation becomes 'live'. In fact, if you are switched on to the attacker's ritual you will not usually even be selected as a victim. This is absolutely the most important factor in 'real' situation and yet it is one area nearly always overlooked by other defence gurus. One aspect of the ritual is the aforementioned four D's, which involve body language as well as the spoken word. This dialogue is often called 'The Interview' (which I will discuss presently). If you can spot the ritual, you can stop the crime.

A part of understanding the enemy is deciphering the language of the street. Much of the attacker's dialogue is used, again innately, as a trigger for violence and to engage a potential victim's brain before assault. Positive interpretation of this 'speak' will unveil signs of imminent assault – literally giving you a countdown to his attack. The ritual alters according to the category of attack, as does the dialogue. I have to make the point before I go on, that none of what you are reading here is or will be of any relevance if the victim is switched off. Deceptive dialogue and cunning entrapments are hardly necessary if the victim is walking across a field at night or down a dark alley in a sparsely populated area. When this is the case – as it very often is – most assaults will be physical and violent almost immediately. The ritual is only used in a bid to trick an intended victim or heighten their vulnerability. If the intended victim has already placed him or herself in a victim state, then they'll be attacked without any warning. To notice rituals and entrapments you have to be switched on and have your eyes wide open otherwise you will suffer the fate of those before you.

If the intent is robbery or rape the dialogue is often disarming or incidental, 'Have you got a light please?' or 'Can you give me directions to Smith St please, I'm a little lost?' The attacker is looking to 'switch the victim off' before attack. In the case of the gratuitous assault where the intent is attack for attack's sake the dialogue is more likely to be aggressive, for example, 'What are you looking at?' In either case the dialogue is employed to gain and distract attention before attack.

Generally speaking, the greater the crime, the greater the deception. At the bottom end of the scale the gratuitous attacker will engage his intended victim with aggressive dialogue, such as, 'I'm gonna batter you, you bastard!' Whilst at the top of the scale the rapist or murderer will prime his victim with anything from a gentlemanly request for directions to, as in the case of killer John Cannan, sending his intended victims, (usually women he had spotted in the street and followed or just met) champagne, flowers and dinner invitations – the ultimate primers for rape and murder. The more cunning attackers drop into the thespian role with Oscar-winning perfection.

This fashion for mindless violence often starts with as little as eye contact. In a volatile environment this can be construed as a subliminal challenge to fight. Many of the fights I witnessed in my time as a nightclub doorman began with the 'eye contact challenge'. You don't have to do any thing wrong to be attacked by this genre of attacker, you just have to be there. Please don't make the mistake of looking for the logic in the attack, there is no logic, the will be no logic and to look for it will only add confusion and indecision. In those seconds of indecision you will have been robbed and beaten – there is no logic.

Most assaults of this nature are, in my opinion, due to displaced aggression. You may trigger off this aggression and become the object of that aggression. Something is pissing these people off in their sad lives. No matter who is trampling on their roses, pissing on their parade, metaphorically kicking the dog when he is down – you will become the object of that pent-up aggression, because you spilled their beer, cut them up in the car, looked at their girlfriend or simply because you were there. That attack is very often brutal, sometimes fatal. Being in Code Yellow will allow you to detect and subsequently avoid these philistines and these incidents in the primary stages, again if you don't know the language you can't talk the lingo.

In the bar or the street you can often spot the gratuitous attacker, he'll have a bad attitude – probably propping up the bar or stalking the dance floor – his elbows pushed out from his sides as though carrying buckets of water. He'll have the customary curled upper lip and will probably be very rude to anyone that moves within a few feet of him. If he's walking down the street he will do so with an overconfident bounce. If he's with others he'll probably be very loud, garrulous and erratic in his movements. He may also be mean and moody with a very aggressive gait. Again, as in the nightclub, he'll be stalking, looking for eye contact. If you are in Code Yellow, you can spot these signs from a mile off.

41

There are two main kinds of eye contact that may escalate into violence:

1) The cursory glance

Someone accidentally catches your eye, or you his. The glance becoming a stare, and progresses to a verbal exchange. This is the pre-cursor to violence. Often, when you make eye contact with someone and it becomes increasingly obvious that you do not know each other, the ego clicks in and goes to work. The initial accidental eye contact becomes a fully-fledged staring contest. The eyes, being a sensitive organ, cannot hold a stare for too long without the occurrence of soreness, watering or blinking. Not wanting to blink first, because it might be construed as a 'backing down', the one with the sorest eyes throws a verbal challenge, ('You fucking looking at me?) to hide the fact that he needs to blink. If the verbal challenge is returned ('Yeah, I am looking at you! What you gonna do about it?'), then the fight is probably on.

To avoid and/or escape the fight scenario, you need to understand the 'cursory glancer'. These are his ritualistic steps:

—   You may catch the eye of someone across a
      crowded room or a street, the look lingers.
—   He asks the question, 'Who are you looking at?'
—   A physical approach follows.
—   He reiterates the question, 'I said, what are you fucking
      looking at?'
—   He then generally progresses to an actual challenge or
      attack. 'Do you wanna 'go', then?'
—   Often the assailant will attack at 'actual challenge'.

—   If he does not, as a pre-cursor to violence, he will often drop into single syllables that act as subliminal action triggers to his attack. Words like 'Yeah', 'And' or 'So' are often employed just before attack. The single syllable is a sure sign that the interview is nearing an end and the introduction of physical violence is imminent.

This is the complete ritual but occasionally, depending upon the victim's response, the attacker may jump steps. For instance he may move directly from the question to the actual challenge, so an early exit is always advisable. I am aware that we are going over old ground here, but it stands repeating. Try and use a physical response only as a last resort. A young man walking down the street alone will think nothing of ignoring a group of barracking men across the road. However, put the man in the same situation and add a female companion, and that man will be ready to argue and fight the world to defend his manhood – even though his lady is begging him not to get involved. These insults mean nothing and should be ignored. As I said earlier 'it's not personal!' Lads, the ladies are not impressed when you walk into a fight that you could have walked out of. I have been involved in many hundreds of fights and can categorically state that it is the stronger man that can walk away, so please walk away, the time to fight is when you are given no alternative. If I have a fight I want it to be for a better reason than, 'the guy was staring at me'. If I end up in court on a manslaughter charge I don't want the judge to be saying to me, 'You killed this man because he spilled you beer Mr Thompson?'

Violence is a serious game, so don't walk into it with any romantic ideas of how it is going to be. It is always ugly and always frightening. I have never stood in front of a man that I wanted to fight, never had perfect conditions and never thought 'Yeah, I'm ready for this'. Every fight for me has been more like, 'I don't want to be here, I don't need this, is this going to be the one that gets me killed or jailed?' Having said all that, and having meant it, if it is going to 'kick off', if you are sure and there is no other way don't hesitate, never allow anyone the opportunity to attack you first. If you can't walk away and you honestly belief that you are going to be attacked, attack first and then get away. The police won't give you this advice, even though it is well within the law, because they probably feel that to sanction violence is to invite it in. They don't want some murder suspect turning up on the front cover of the national newspapers saying, 'I only did what PC Dick told me to do.'

Perhaps the police are frightened of the consequences of honesty, believing the general populace do not have the intelligence to handle lawfully defending themselves. One PC, (I have actually heard several reports of this happening at police-run courses for nightclub doormen), told one of my friends, that he could not legally attack first and must wait to be attacked and then counter-attack, with reasonable force, if he wanted to stay within the law. Now, forgive me if I overreact here, but that is not just bad advice, it is untrue. The law allows pre-emptive behaviour, as long as it fits with the circumstances: you truly believe that you are about to be attacked. I will deal with this in more detail in a later chapter.

In the case of the cursory glancer, it is advisable not to hold eye contact. If you are sure that it is just a cursory glance and not a challenging stare (it will usually be very obvious) just smile, perhaps say, 'hello' and then break the eye contact. This will probably leave him thinking; 'Oh I must know him, where do I know him from?' The ritual is then broken at the very first stage. If he does ask you what you are looking at, just apologise and say that you thought he looked familiar. If he asks you if you want trouble say 'no'. This will usually end the confrontation because he will feel as though he has won and wander off to his cave. This will be hard if you are a male with an ego to feed, but a lot easier if you are a confident person that does not need to hurt people to prove your masculinity. Women rarely have a problem with submissiveness. Unless a woman has been brought up with a weak male role model it is not normally in her nature to be the 'protector'. If the latter is the case, she may have developed male characteristics to balance the loss in her environment, one of those characteristics being the ego. If you are still approached put up a 'fence' (to be detailed) and prepare for a physical encounter.

2) Eye contact challenger

Firstly, In the case of the eye contact challenger, if you sense a rowdy individual/s walk tall and hold yourself confidently. Even if you do feel daunted, act confidently – after all 'when ignorance is mutual, confidence is King'. Confident people are very rarely chosen as victims for attack. Whenever possible, avoid eye contact where you sense aggression, but do not bow your head, this can be seen as a sign of weakness and may draw the attacker in for the kill. The challenger's ritual can be crushed before it starts by simply avoiding eye contact, if you are switched on you will have noticed him from a mile off and avoidance will not be a problem. This may take some discipline, it is often difficult not to stare, because you feel almost drawn to something that you should not look at. Practice by sitting facing the TV and trying to avoid looking at it for 2 minutes. You might not find that it is not as easy as you thought. If you do not make eye contact then you have avoided a situation.

If eye contact has already occurred, break the engagement immediately and quickly separate yourself from the aggressor by as great a distance as possible. If this proves fruitless and aggressive verbal exchange ensues, do not retaliate, just walk away, a verbal counter may act as a catalyst. If you do not or cannot decamp at this stage and are approached, prepare for 'fight or flight'. Only fight if there is no other option open to you.

Returning the verbal challenge

Retaliation, however justified, will be seen by your aggressor as an acceptance to fight. From my experience, if you do not make a hasty retreat at, 'actual challenge', especially if you do counter verbally, more threats and a possibly attack will result. A non-counter and immediate exit on the part of the victim usually results in the challenger aborting, perceiving the response, or lack thereof, to be an embryonic victory. Therefore, if a verbal challenge is thrown do not counter.

If you are approached and are unable to escape, then you must prepare yourself for fight or flight. If you are in a pub and you sense trouble, it is my advice to leave that particular pub and find another that feels less threatening. An ounce of prevention is better than a pound of cure. At and before eye contact you should have been in Code Yellow, this will have given you awareness, not only of the potential situation, but also of the 'ritual'. In such situations knowledge is power.

Like a cancer, confrontation should be caught and treated as early as possible – the longer you leave it, the graver it will become. It is easier to treat a small malignancy than a fully-grown tumour. If a verbal challenge is thrown down, you should rise with the threat to Code Orange where a potency assessment may be made. If an approach follows you should automatically rise to Code Red, this being 'fight or flight'. The approach may be made across the bar of a public house, on the street, in a traffic incident, it may be some one getting out of their car and approaching your vehicle. At this stage you should have already utilised your 'flight' option and be a hundred yards down the road. Where 'flight' may not be plausible you may take advantage of the aforementioned Four D's, if this technique works for your attacker then it can work for you. As the famous Japanese strategist Miyomoto Musashi said in his *Book of Five Rings*; 'What is true for one is true for a thousand and what is true for a thousand is true for ten thousand.' In other words, if it works against you it can also work for you.

We now move on to the professional attacker who works for profit and covets compliance. He does not want to fight. To make his job easier he employs guile as opposed to force, this coming via deception. As with all predators, he seeks people in a victim state, or Code White. He is usually very different from the archetypal, celluloid attacker that we have been programmed to expect. This is the case with the most disarming of predators. They rarely look like potential attackers. The archetypal stocking-faced robber with a cosh and a swag bag is far removed from the real world villain who is more likely to be dressed in a smart suit and tie.

As with most attacks the professional attacker follows a ritual, understanding this is the pre-requisite to threat avoidance. There appear to be four different kinds of mugger:

1)   The 'snatch and run' mugger, who literally rips your handbag/briefcase from your shoulder/hand and runs away at speed, or even drives away on a bike.
2)   The blind side mugger who suddenly appears out of an entry without any apparent warning
3)   The defiant mugger who attacks without ritual or fear of the law or consequences, usually because you have walked into his patch or have inadvertently crossed his path and he wants whatever you have got
4)   The professional mugger who plans his attacks and uses deception as a 'way in'.

Environmental awareness is the best way to avoid the first three, but a thorough understanding of attack ritual is the only real way of avoiding the fourth. Below are the ritualistic steps of the latter. If you can spot the ritual in the early stages you can avoid attack. Attackers look for victims, and the ideal victim is in Code White, mentally and/or environmentally: those daydreaming or detached from the herd. Selection often occurs in sparsely populated locations, the mugger wanting as little fuss as possible in the execution of his attack. He favours the quiet park/street/entry etc. This does not mean that people are safe in highly populated areas like shopping malls or busy streets. Very often the mugger stalks such places for victims, after selection following them to a safe attack zone like the car park. It is thought that Stephanie Slater, murdered by Cannan, was stalked in just such a way. Cannan spotted her in a shopping centre and followed her to the car park, which was his trade mark, pouncing as she got into her car.

Prior to attack a stalking of the chosen victim often occurs, like a cheetah stalking an antelope. This is a part of priming. If necessary the victim will be followed in the hope that he/she will heighten their vulnerability mentally/environmentally by walking into a park, down a quiet street/entry etc. If the victim is followed from a shopping mall the attacker often waits for him/her to put the shopping in the boot of the car or even strike as he/she enters the car. It is at such times that even normally vigilant people drop their guard, and even though it may only be for a second, this is all the attacker needs.

When you have your hands full of shopping and are trying to get the kids into the car you may not notice that you are being followed. Often the attacker covers the whole of a car park without being noticed. His attack is then so swift that even other people in the car park do not notice what has happened. When you are off-loading the shopping and getting into the car, be very aware. As soon as you are in the car, bang the locks on immediately.

Often if the attacker needs more information he will initiate an exploratory approach, coupled with disarming dialogue. It is also used as a secondary awareness assessment – the attacker wants to see if you are switched on, wants to make sure he is safe before he attacks. If at this point, or at any point after victim stalking, the victim appears switched off, the mugger may initiate his threatened attack without further priming. Unless the attacker is a real pro he will show signs of adrenal reaction in the exploratory approach that you will sense. Listen to your instincts.

If the attacker feels that the chosen victim is switched onto the attempt and his secondary assessment is negative, he will often abort and find a more vulnerable victim. If he feels that the chosen victim is switched off he may initiate the attack/threatened attack whilst the victim is engaged in answering his disarming question – this may be any thing from asking directions to asking the time. Often the disarming question will switch off those that are switched on. An experienced attacker will use deception to take down any defensive fences that his intended victims may have put up.

The professional attacker often likes to take his booty without actually attacking his victim, instead he threatens to attack. I found it very interesting that many of the muggers that I interviewed used the 'threatened attack' as opposed to the 'actual attack' to prime their victims. They professed that this was because if they got caught and they had used violence in the course of the attack, the sentence they got would be longer because of it. So they frightened victims into submission, rather than beat them into supplication.

The mugger will often threaten the victim with attack to frighten them in to supplication, frequently underlining the threat with a weapon or an accomplice, or both. These threats will be aggressive and menacing, thus effecting adrenal dump in the victim, quickly escalating to the freeze syndrome (the reasoning process mistakes adrenaline for fear, often freezing victims into immobility). The threats are repeated with escalating aggression causing the victim to experience multiple adrenal release, grossly heightening the supposed feeling of fear and adding to the 'freeze'. The threats of course are married with demands for money/credit cards etc.

Often the attacker threatens to hurt the victim if they are not compliant, or, not to hurt the victim in exchange for compliance. It is not uncommon for attackers to use a physical attack, creating compliance via disablement, others initiate an attack to disable the victim, before robbing them. Sometimes the attack will be minimal, used only to add to 'freeze', on other occasions, the attack will be frenzied and severe. Any chance of a physical defence, other than actually attacking back with the same degree (or greater) of ferocity, is unlikely to be effective. The concepts of 'blocking' an assailant's blows or using hypothesised 'release' techniques are unsound. If the situation has got this far, only the very strong will survive.

If you know how the bad guys work it stands to reason that you can avoid him like the plague. These people mainly rely on deception, not so easy now that you know how the blighters work. Avoid at all costs, escape as soon as you see their ritual in play, if that doesn't work, or the option has been spent then use verbal dissuasion.

Chapter Three

Verbal Dissuasion

When avoidance is gone and escape is no longer possible we are left with verbal dissuasion. Verbal dissuasion means talking the situation down. There is not a lot to say here that isn't obvious, other than the fact that you should never undertake mediation without some sort of protective shield, that shield is what I call 'the fence'. Now the fence is a whole subject in its own right and should be studied in-depth. For this I recommend that you read my book, or watch my video; *The Fence*. I shall give you a brief outline of it here because, as I said it is very dangerous to start negotiations without a fence and a book on avoidance tactics cannot be complete without its inclusion.

Therefore, as soon as you are approached in a potentially confrontational situation take up a small forty five degree stance (as illustrated) by moving your right (or left) leg inconspicuously behind you. Simultaneously splay your arms (fence), as though in exclamation, whilst replying with your dialogue. The lead hand is placed between you and the assailant, the reverse hand back, ready to control or attack. As you will see in the illustrations, the fence allows you to control the distance between you and your attacker, disabling any attempts he may make at grabbing/striking you. Though it may be on a subconscious level, your fence will act as a barrier between you and he. Try not to touch the assailant with your hands, unless you are forced to, the touch may fuel the fire and possibly result in your wrists being grabbed. If he keeps forcing forward, you are in danger, attack is certainly imminent so make your decision without haste. Indecision begets defeat.

For the duration of dialogue it is imperative to maintain distance control until you are able to escape, or are forced or strike. If you are forced into an attack situation – this should be an absolute last resort – make it a telling blow to a vulnerable area. Explode into the opponent with every fibre of your being, then run!! Many defence gurus advocate a second strike, a finisher. If there is a choice in the matter, don't do it. The few seconds you buy with your first strike could easily be lost if you linger for even a second. With some of the people I have interviewed, and certainly in many of the incidents I have witnessed, this attempted and unnecessary *coup de grace* resulted in the victim being grabbed, and subsequently defeated. There is also the danger of your attacker's accomplices (if he has any), coming to his aid if you do not take advantage and beat a hasty retreat. So unless a second strike is absolutely necessary the rule of thumb is 'hit and run'.

The Art of Fighting Without Fighting

Dissuasion range, or conversation range usually allows only 8-12 inches between you and your potential opponent. If this is mismanaged it rapidly degenerates into vertical grappling range and then ground fighting – not a good place to be if you don't know the arena or are facing more than one opponent. Whilst conversation distance is not the chosen range of the majority – most people feel safer at about 4 or 5 feet – it can be maintained so that it does not degenerate further into grappling range by 'putting a fence around your factory'.

If you had a factory that you wanted to protect from robbers, the most sensible thing to do would be to place a fence around it to make it a hard target. Therefore a potential robber has got to get past that fence before he can even think about attacking the factory. Whilst the fence might not keep him out indefinitely it will make his job decidedly harder. Rather like a boxer who constantly flicks a jab into his opponent's face, even if that jab does not hurt his opponent it keeps him at bay. If his opponent wants to employ his Knock Out blow he first has to find away past his opponent's jab-to the boxer the jab is the fence around his factory.

In practical terms the 'fence around your factory' is your lead hand, placed in that all-important space between you and your antagonist to maintain a safe gap. Like the factory fence the lead hand will not keep an aggressor at bay for ever –just long enough for you to initiate verbal dissuasion, escape or a pre-emptive attack – but it will place you in charge, even though your aggressor may not know it. Placed correctly the lead hand will not only maintain a safe gap, but it will also disable the attacker's armoury (right and left-hand techniques/ head butt etc). Although the aggressor may not realise this on a conscious level, he will instinctively understand that, until that fence has been removed or by-passed, his techniques have no clear way through.

The lead hand should be held in a non-aggressive way and should not touch the aggressor unless he makes a forward movement and tries to bridge the gap between you and he.

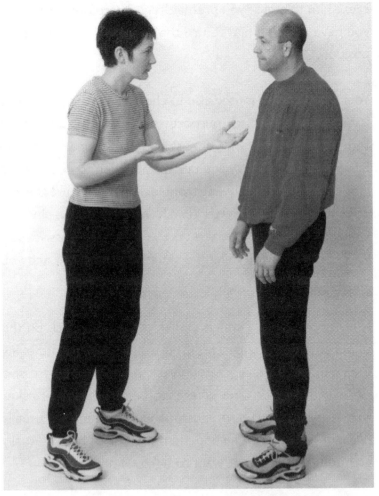

The lead hand acts as an antenna to your aggressor's intentions. If he moves forward, he will touch the fence and set your alarm bells ringing. This forward movement should be checked so as to maintain the safe range by using the palm of the lead hand on the aggressor's chest. Don't hold the touch, as this may be seen by your assailant as a controlling movement. Whilst of course it is a controlling action, it's better, at this stage that the aggressor does not feel that you are in control, this creates a power play and may force him to knock your hand away or grab your wrist and possibly cause him to attack you prematurely. Therefore, as soon as you have checked him return the lead hand to its stand-by position.

Your reverse hand is used also to check range but primarily it is held back for attack purposes should the dissuasion fail and you find an attack you last line of defence. Once the fence is up, you can try and talk the attacker down by telling him that you do not want trouble. This may hurt the old pride a little, but it is better than having to become physical. Depending upon your make-up you can be submissive with your speak or if you think the situation demands it and you can carry it off, firm to aggressive.

It is important, as I stated earlier to keep a check on the opponent's body language. If he is aggressive and moving forward then he is a greater threat than if he is aggressive and standing back. The difference being that the attacker that is moving forward and touching the fence is usually preparing to attack. The opponent that stands back is usually posturing and does not want to become physical.

Below are some of the physical traits that might give the attacker's intent away. Running concurrently with attack ritual will be signs of adrenal reaction this attack body language which, if spotted, can help you to recognise potential menace. It has to be said though, that many of the very experienced attackers may have learned to hide adrenal reaction and only an expert eye will see imminent attack.

Erratic eye movement

The attacker or his accomplice, concerned about being caught mid-act, will constantly be checking for police/general public involvement. Whilst he is speaking to you his eyes will be darting in other directions. Therefore it is a bad sign if he keeps looking past and around you as he speaks.

Adrenal reaction

Unless the attacker is seasoned he will be showing signs of adrenaline. His face will appear pale his eyes wide from adrenaline-induced tunnel vision, he will be stern and unsmiling. He may also fidget in an attempt to hide 'adrenal shake' (the body will ' shiver' as though cold) and his voice may have a nervous quiver.

Arm splaying

The attacker's arms will splay in a fit of exclamation. This is an innate way of making him appear physically bigger before attack.

Finger beckoning

The attacker will often beckon his victim on with his fingers.

Head nodding

The assailant may sporadically nod his head.

Neck Pecking

He will peck his neck like a cockerel usually in conjunction with his single syllable challenge and to protect the throat.

Eye bulge

Due the tunnel vision that accompanies adrenaline, the attacker's eyes may appear wide and staring.

Dropped eyebrows

The eyebrows drop before attack to protect the eyes.

Stancing up

He will often turn sideways on and take up an innate fighting stance, thus hiding his major organs from attack.

Distance close-down

With every passing second of the altercation, the attacker will advance closer to his victim, his movements and tone becoming more erratic and aggressive the closer he gets to actual attack.

Hand concealment

If the attacker is carrying a weapon, the bearing hand may be hidden, either in his pocket or behind his back. If one – or both – of his hands is concealed, beware. Some attackers do not hide the hands, rather they turn the palm or palms away from the chosen victim on approach to conceal a weapon, or keep the offending hand close to their leg to conceal the same. Other attackers will keep their hands on full display, extracting a weapon from its hiding place as they approach, or immediately after asking an engaging question.

My friend was killed in just such a way. His attacker approached with his right palm turned into his right thigh so that his knife was hidden. He got very close to my friend and asked a question to distract him, then he plunged the hidden knife into his heart. That single stab wound killed him. So look out for concealment, if you can't see the attacker's hands or if his palm is turned in or even if the attacker has his hand in his pocket, you have to ask yourself why. It is very likely that he is concealing a weapon. Cannan used to carry an old carrier bag in which he kept a number of dangerous weapons. When he asked his intended victim a question, again as a distraction, he would reach into his bag and take out his implement.

If the approach is made by more than one person they will all usually display the same physical traits.

Pincer movement

If more than one assailant is involved, it is usual for one of them to deploy the victim with distracting dialogue whilst the other/s move to your off side. Whilst the victim is distracted by the questioner, his accomplice/s attack. This was one of the most common attacks in the nightclub when I worked as a doorman and is a common, though, unbelievably, innate, ploy of gang robbery or rapes.

The reason that so many people seem to get glassed or stabbed in the side of the face or neck, is because they are not attacked by the person in front that they are arguing with. Instead, they are attacked from the side by someone who they do not see, because of their adrenal-induced tunnel vision.

The Art of Fighting Without Fighting

As stated earlier most aggression in society is probably due to displacement. It's not personal so don't let it become personal. Similarly, there is no room in any kind of life-threatening situation for ego – all the ego will do is get you into trouble. I had a friend who was out in the park with his wife and baby daughter. The child was in a pushchair. It was a lovely summer's day and there were a lot of people wandering around the park. Just a normal Sunday afternoon really. He didn't even notice the three skinheads sizing him up about 100 yards in front (avoidance) and by the time he was fully aware of their presents they already had the Stanley knife out and were threatening to 'cut' his daughter if he didn't hand over his wallet. He told me that, about a minute before they initiated their threat, he had noticed them approach and had the chance to make a hasty retreat in the opposite direction, he actually felt like grabbing his family and running away but thought that cowardly. No, he couldn't allow himself to do that. Why? Because his ego wouldn't allow it. He felt that he had to stay put, like the hunter-gatherer he was conditioned to think he was, and protect his family.

By listening to his ego he lost any real chance of getting out the situation in tact. Part of the reason the lad had such an over-developed ego was the fact that he was a high Danned martial artist. Physically the lad was a phenomenon, but mentally he was ill-prepared for this kind of confrontation. As he said to me himself, 'my bottle went'. Actually his bottle didn't go. I've never met anyone that ever lost their bottle, just people that were tricked by their lack of adrenal understanding. It is our instinct as human being to run not to fight, unless cornered and left no other option. Do you think our mammalian ancestors would have had any problem running away from a sabre-toothed tiger? Do you think that they may have worried about what their friends would have thought if they didn't defend their honour by standing and fighting? I don't think so. All they would have been concerned about was getting the hell out of there, by any, and the fastest means possible. In fact their senses would have been so honed that they would have noticed the modern day sabre-toothed tiger, the skin head, long before the attack and escaped before there was even a confrontation.

The Freeze Syndrome

topple

I know that it's easy to say in hindsight, but my friend should have seen the threat and avoided it by over-riding his ego. He should have gone the opposite way, or made a run for it when avoidance was no longer an option, or talked down his attackers if faced with a confrontation. Unfortunately, he couldn't talk it down, he was so unused to the amount of adrenaline that it caused 'freeze syndrome', and he became monosyllabic. He gave his wallet over without an argument because he was lost for words and felt terror like he had never felt it before. All he wanted was for the encounter to end, so that he could be safe again. Afterwards of course he fell into a terrible depression because he felt that he had let his wife and his daughter down by not defending them. He also felt that he had let himself and his martial art down. The lad was carrying the world on his shoulders. He had never let his wife down, or himself, in fact he had never let anyone down before. Although he was unaware of this, his body reacted exactly the way it was designed to react, it prepared him for flight. That was the best option open to him, but contemporary peer pressure, ego, morality don't comprehend this logic and wouldn't allow it. He had to stay and meet this threat.

Our bodies our designed with a survival mechanism that does not take into consideration what others might think about our actions, only what is right for survival of the species. That's why we have the 95% rule. At times of confrontation 95% of us (the other 5% are classed as sociopaths) will have the instinct to run away to protect the evolution of the species. We won't know this on a conscious level of course, we'll only know that we want to run and not why. This is where the downward spiral of self-doubt begins and subsequently, in the aftermath the self-esteem falls flatter than a shadow.

Going back to the pub story with my mate the 6th Dan, escape for him was as simple as walking out of the door to go to another bar where the threat was not so prevalent. But he couldn't do that because he reasoned that he had as much right to stand and drink in that shit hole as any one else. Anyway, what would his mates think if he backed down from this potential confrontation? They'd think he was scared that's what they'd think. As you can see, this is all ego play. It is not the sign of a mentally developed martial artist, nor is it really his fault because he is no different from many of the other high graded martial artists – it is the fault of a system that teaches only the physical response. It is also the fault of the grading system that elevates the Dan grades to almost God-like status.

Higher grades in most traditional systems are revered, nay worshiped. This reverence doesn't squash the negative emotions in the way that the martial arts are supposed to – in fact it does quite the opposite – it enlarges the ego and encourages many of the negatives that we should be driving out like demons. So we end up with a very high graded, very capable (physically) martial artist that is stuck to a pub bar by the superglue of peer pressure and ignorance. If a bar is threatening, go to a different bar and fuck what any one else might think about it or you. They say it is a strong man that can walk away – there was never a truer statement. Your ippon should never be defending a space by the bar, or a bit of tarmac on the road. Your ippon should be over-riding all the non-starters and escaping if the circumstances allow. If you can't escape, verbal dissuasion is the next line of defence and also incorporates escape. We are employing verbal to escape a potentially violent situation.

Have at you sir!

Do your worst you rotter!

Two prime males prepare to defend their space at the bar. What finer sight can there be?

If you are walking down the street and you sense malice in front of you, walk the other way or cross the street, nip into a busy shop, stop a policeman or knock on a house door and ask them to call the police. If you're in a bar and you sense that there is going to be trouble inform the doorstaff, escape out the back exit, phone the police etc. If you are forced into verbal dissuasion, then communication is of the utmost importance. You have to be able to talk your way out of conflict. This is not so easy when you consider that a great deal of blood is drawn away from the brain during fight or flight and pumped to the muscular areas involved in behavioural release (physical action). This lack of blood in the brain often leaves the recipient unable to talk in sentences and often unable to talk at all. Not good if you need to employ verbal dissuasion. Even for those that do manage to talk the voice often quivers fearfully for all to hear, this is not good if you are trying to convey a message of confidence. The only way to overcome this disability is to practice by placing yourself in fearful situations, ones manufactured in the controlled arena or life confrontations, and practice speaking whilst under the influence of adrenaline.

Before my students took place in animal day sessions I would get them to converse with each other so that they can learn to raise their voices above the voice tremors and practice voice control. It works. If you want to get used to the water, get your trunks on and get wet. Hypothesising for an eternity won't get you used to the feel – you get used to the sensation by 'feeling' .

Loopholing

If someone approaches you aggressively and accuses you of 'staring' at them, even if you haven't don't be afraid to apologise if you think that it might get you out of a violent confrontation. It doesn't have to be sycophantic, it doesn't have to be weak, it can simply be a statement like, 'I wasn't aware that I was staring at you, if I was then I'm sorry.' End of story. If you felt that the energy was right you could even say it aggressively, to let him feel you intent. This would be loopholing, what I call giving the opponent and honourable way out of the situation. I can say 'sorry' to a man in such a way that it will frighten the crap out of him, but it will still be loopholing, because he can go back to his mates or girlfriend without losing face and say 'Yeah, well he apologised, lucky for him. If he didn't I have done him.' I used to take people to one side, away from their mates, and place my arm around them and tell them quietly that if they didn't fuck off and quick I was going to hammer them in front of their mates. As the potential aggressor was moving back to his mates, I'd pat him on the back in a friendly manner so that I didn't look like the aggressor. The lad could then go back to his friends and tell them what ever he liked to save face, and they' d believe it because I was not aggressive.

The One in Ten Rule

One of my friends, a veteran street fighter used what he called the 'one in ten rule'. His theory (and he made it work many times) was that if you can find the leader of a gang of ten men, and control him, then you automatically controlled the other nine.

He was a pub landlord and whenever he took over a new pub he'd find out over the first few weeks who the ring leader was, who played up, who was chancing their arm as it were. Once he knew he would choose the right moment and separate the one from the ten and take him into the cellars saying that he had a proposition. Once in the cellars he would lock the door and offer the guy a 'square go', a match fight. Due to my friend's fearsome reputation as a fighter, they would invariably bottle it at this point and he'd warn then never to cross him again. He knew that the ring leader was in danger of losing face in front of his mates so, as they came out of the cellar and back into the bar, he would overtly make a fuss of the guy – arm round the shoulder and free pint from behind the bar. This meant that the lad could go back to his mates and they'd be none the wiser as to what had gone on. Only he and the gaffer would know, and that was enough because once he had control of the one he had control of the ten.

I loopholed a lot when I worked as a nightclub doorman. If a guy was looked as though he might start trouble I'd pull him to one side and say, 'Hey man don't you respect me? I thought we were friends?'

'Yeah I respect you, but that wanker over there ... I'm gonna kill him.'

'Listen,' I'd continue, 'if you respect me then don't fight in my place. You know I run this door and you shouldn't fight in here. Now do me a favour and leave it out.'

With this the fellow would walk back to his mates and tell them how he was letting the guy off because Geoff Thompson had asked him to do so as a personal favour to him. That's the loophole: he doesn't really want to fight anyway, so I'm giving him a way out, he just need something that he could tell his mates.

Most people, despite their posturing and loud mouthing, don't really want to be in a fight. Again the 95% Rule applies – 95% of the people don't want to fight and if you give them a half-decent reason not to, especially an honourable excuse, then they'll take it.

Chapter Four

Posturing

Posturing is the all but lost art of beating people by means of psyche, winning with guile as opposed to force. It is the art of fighting without fighting. In layman's terms it means scaring the shit out of the opponent with 'blag', so that they don't want to enter a physical arena with you. For every fight that I've had where I employed a physical response, I must have had at least another three where I beat my opponent with posturing techniques, guile as opposed to force. Initially, in my early days of door work I postured instinctively, though not very convincingly. Then, when I realised the potency of the long forgotten art of posturing, I started to explore the histrionics of it and then, subsequently fine tune it until it became laser sharp. Whenever a potentially confrontational situation arose on the door I would practice posturing to see if I could psyche the opponent out instead of knocking him out. I had great success with it, now it is my teaching mainstay.

I generally employ posturing when verbal dissuasion is not working. You can usually tell when this occurs because the attacker will keep moving forward and touching the fence – a very bad sign. Distance close down is one of the final pre-cursors to a physical attack. I never let any one touch the fence more than twice – it's too dangerous.

Firstly let me explain why posturing works and where the premise for the 95% rule was formed. There have been numerous surveys carried out on soldiers in wartime, which reveal that in most conflicts, bar the Vietnam War (I'll discuss that later) – at the point of actually killing another human being, even at the threat of being killed themselves – 95% of the soldiers became conscientious objectors. That is, at the point of actually killing another person of the same species 95% of the people couldn't do it. They shot their bullets into the ground, high into the air or they didn't shoot at all. Hence the need for a sergeant kicking the soldiers up the arse and making them kill. So 5% of the soldiers did approximately 95% of the killings. These soldiers are generally classed by society as sociopaths, people that have no problem killing others of the same species. This is similar to the way the immune system sends out killer T-cells to kill cancerous or viral cells entering the body. The other 95% of cells in the body are not designed to kill, instead they are designed to help sustain life.

What the 95% Rule tells us, is that in violent conflicts of a self-defence nature (eg. street fights), 95% of the people are going to react in exactly the same way. As in warfare between nations, the same rules apply to a small conflict between two people, or any situation that the brain sees as contentious. This is a war in microcosm – a small war. So 95% of us, when faced with conflict, are not going to want to be there, we too are going to become conscientious objectors. What this fact allows us to comprehend, is that the majority of people don't want to fight and if we can give them any way out they, and we, will take it. The instinct to run as opposed to fight, as stated earlier, is deeply imbedded in our genes and goes back to mammalian ancestry. Our instinct in that dangerous age was sharply honed for survival at any cost, this usually meant fleeing from wild animals that wanted to eat us and were to big/dangerous to fight against. Fortunately (or unfortunately, depending upon your views), these instincts are still with us, though we have lost our understanding of them somewhat. If we flee from potential danger in this age, especially the male of the species, we feel –or we are made to feel – like cowards.

The instinct to run is deeply embedded.

Therefore, when faced by danger, 95% of us want to run away. This feeling is not easily overridden, it is so strong that most of us will flee before we even know what has happened to us. This is because when we are in fight or flight mode, we revert to what is called the mid-brain, and in mid-brain we are hardly discernible from animals.

My friend was telling me how disgusted he was by the actions of several men who displayed 'cowardly' tendencies in a 'virtual reality' ride that he went on in London. This virtual reality war game involved a group being locked in a room and exposed to a pretend war scenario. Several men were in the room with their girlfriends and wives eagerly anticipating the fun, when suddenly the doors burst open and some soldiers burst in with automatic weapons (part of the game) and opened fire. Three of the men, going into mid-brain, ran for the door in an attack of panic, one even elbowed his girl friend in the face to escape. Their brains thought that the danger was real and thousands of years of instinct locked into their genes went into action. They fled for their lives. I explained to my horrified friend that these men did nothing more than react to natural instinct. Believe me, no-one will be feeling as bad as these men, who will be sitting at home beating themselves up, wondering why they are such cowards. It takes great understanding and will to override these very strong instincts.

During the Vietnam War the soldiers were taught to override natural instinct and, as a consequence, the 95% rule was reversed – 95% of the soldiers did kill. This reversal was due to the psychological training that the soldiers were put through. The American soldiers went through a period of desensitisation and dehumanisation: they watched video footage of the Viet Cong acting out atrocities – killing, butchering, raping women and children – until they no longer saw their enemy as human beings, rather they viewed them as animals. When they shot at the Vet Cong they were merely shooting rats on a river bank. It is slightly peripheral to this book, but I have to say that dehumanisation, in my opinion is not a good thing, it is used here only to give example to my point.

The Art of Fighting Without Fighting

Our 'ancestral instinct', is badly outdated and has gone crazy in a society where we have more neurological stressors than ever before. The fight or flight instinct works off the senses and triggers adrenaline and other stress hormones, such as Cortisol, when it feels that danger is imminent. In theory this seems fine, it prepares us for a life or death battles with contemporary aggressors. In reality though this is not the case because our senses are constantly being attacked by stimuli that 'might' be aggressive but most often are not. Even the aggressive horn of a car can trigger 'fight or flight', releasing a cocktail of stress hormones into the blood for a behavioural release that never occurs. Moving jobs, moving house, changing partners, confronting the boss etc. may cause us enough worry to fool the brain into thinking that the intangible threat is in fact a sabre-toothed tiger, releasing adrenaline that is not utilised behaviourally. Of course these things are not life and death scenarios, but our senses think that they are and still give us the instinct to run away, which a greater majority do and so never achieve their life's dreams. People often don't take chances in their life, career, relationship or hobby because they feel this mammalian instinct to run for their lives. Fear is what keeps people ordinary. Humans, as a species, do not realise their potential, because fear acts as a barrier between them and their dreams. We are also left with the very corrosive effect of Cortisol remaining in the blood stream when behavioural fight or flight was not actuated.

Cortisol, one of the main chemicals released during fight or flight, has a very corrosive effect on the soft muscle tissue like the heart, lungs and intestines. It is also thought to play a part in inadvertently killing brain cells. So if we have physiological fight or flight (the release of stress hormones) but no behavioural fight or flight (those same stress hormones are not used and stay in the blood, like tissue assassins), we are killing ourselves from the inside out. The body realises this and will find any surrogate release it can for these trapped hormones, usually in a displaced manner, for example road rage, marital disputes, temper tantrums, irrational behaviour, even violence. These incidents do release the trapped hormones but, due to the contentious nature of the release, they create more and we find ourselves locked into a cycle of stress degeneration. Let me explain: you take your stress out on a family member, perhaps your wife, she gets in a mood with you and doesn't speak for two days. What does that do? It creates more stress because there is contention in the home. I could go on all day about this but I am already aware that I have slipped outside the context of this book. So for more details on this please refer to my books *Fear – The Friend of Exceptional People* and *The Other Side of Fear*.

The Fence
So, back to the script. If, for whatever reason, you find yourself in front of a potential attacker who is constantly touching the fence and giving you signs that an attack is imminent and you can't bring yourself to attack pre-emptively, then you need to create a gap between you and him and take the fence to a conscious level. That means that he will realise that you are taking control. If he is trying to bridge the gap and take down the fence, but you are not prepared to attack then you MUST take the fence to a conscious level or you are facing grave danger. The fence will be crushed and you attacked as a consequence.

The Art of Fighting Without Fighting

It is important with the conscious fence to create a gap –
about 5 feet would be good – between you and the assailant.
You can do this by stepping back (or pushing him back if you
can' t step back for some reason) away from the attacker,
whilst simultaneously using your lead hand to shove the
attacker so that he also goes back. You can also create a gap
by using a slap and step back, a two handed shove or a Thai
leg kick. Any approach will do, as long as after the contact
you create a gap between you and he.

The intention of the shove (or whatever device you use) is
to trigger adrenaline in your opponent, thus hopefully
triggering his 'flight response', making him feel the urge to
want to run away. By triggering the adrenaline you
automatically trigger the 95% Rule. So, if the situation has
reached an impasse and you think it is going to become
physical, but you do not want to attack him for whatever
reason, then shove him hard in the chest, knocking him
backwards and out of immediate attacking range. This minimal
physical contact will cause an adrenal release in the opponent.
Back the shove up with a very aggressive verbal fence, 'Stay
there, don't ****ing move!' Use expletives to add intent and
aggression. I feel that this is important because it is the 'speak'
of the street. If you were to say 'Damn well stay there you
cad!' it would be devoid of weight and the attacker would
probably laugh you off the planet. Speak in his language or he
won't understand you.

The reasons for the gap are manifold, not least because it
takes the opponent out of his striking range. What it also
does is take the opponent from a state of reaction to a state
of response – from 'fight' response to 'flight' response. Let

74

me explain: if you shove the opponent, but not out of range, he may automatically react to the shove with a counter-shove, or an attack, of his own. He'll do this without even thinking because it is an automatic reaction. Whilst in fight or flight mode we are in what is known as 'mid-brain', and in mid-brain we are hardly discernible from animals. Our prime objective in mid-brain is survival, and if that means running away that is what our instinct will get us to do. In effect, by staying within strike range you are forcing the opponent into a 'fight' response, and he will react like a cornered animal. His instincts (which will have been in his genes through many, many generations) will inform him that he is cornered and that he should 'fight his way out'. (This is not a good thing for obvious reasons.) If however you shove him out of attack range you will trigger his 'flight' response and give him the instinct to run or freeze because he is no longer a cornered animal, so there is no longer a reason to fight. He won't even know this on a conscious level, but thousands of years of instinct will inform him that he is no longer cornered and he should run for his very life. Even if he does not run away, the fact that he feels like running away will create confusion and self-doubt triggering more adrenaline and a downward spiral to capitulation.

Once you have created a gap (and the confusion) the opponent is forced out of attack mode and into escape mode. The only way that he is going to be able to override this very strong emotion is to consciously disregard all natural instincts and move forward. Not an easy task, especially if the adversary is not an experienced one. This very often effects what I like to call the 'sticky feet syndrome'. The attacker may very well want to move forward because peer pressure demands that he fight and not run away, but his feet appear stuck to the floor, his body lurches forward as though trying to move, but his feet stay stuck firmly to the ground. This is because natural instinct is telling him to run for it.

After creating the gap make yourself a hard target by 'ballooning', or 'stalking'. This is done by pacing left to right without taking your eyes off the opponent, at the same time you shout out verbal commands like, 'stay there, don't move!' and point to the opponent, this acts as a secondary back up fence to the verbal.

Interestingly the ballooning also triggers innate instincts within the opponent that go right back to the dawn of mammalian man, when we were not at the top of the food chain and were prey to bigger animals. Your antagonist will literally feel as though he is being 'stalked' before attack. The thought that he is being hunted like a wild beast will serve to increase his woe. If you watch the cheetah when it hunts the antelope, he balloons (or stalks) just before the attack – in fact most animals do, we are no exception. It can be used by us as an attacking tool to trick the opponent into a flight response, or against us – often inadvertently – to effect the same 'freeze' or 'flight' tendencies.

There are many kinds of fence.

Back your ballooning up with a physical fence, pointing, and a verbal fence in the form of strong commands like, 'Keep away from me, stay where you are!' If you make this loud

The Art of Fighting Without Fighting

and aggressive and splay your arms erratically this would be classed as 'posturing'. Posturing is the art of fighting without fighting. This is what animals do in nature, generally with animals of their own species. Rather than fight and kill each other and thus threaten the survival of their own species, they posture by making themselves as big and as aggressive as possible, thus triggering the flight response in their opponent, defeating them without injury. Watch the cat when he faces the dog, his back rises, his eyes glare, he hisses aggressively. He looks ferocious. The cat makes himself as big and aggressive as possible to try and frighten the dog away.

I recommend that you take advantage of your opponent's reaction to you posturing and make your get away as soon as possible. We have already spoken about the adrenal syndrome, how it can effect the human body and how the reasoning process mistakes adrenaline for fear, thus triggering the 'flight' response. By giving an opponent an adrenal release, we trigger the natural instinct to either freeze or run. Both of these would have been very natural defences against pre-historic beasts that were too fearsome to stand and fight or whose eyesight was poor and would not be able to see a frozen enemy, only attacking when they sensed movement. In this society 'freezing' or 'running' is not always an option and may only get you battered by an antagonist that will use a frozen adversary as a punch bag. Society is not kind either to the fellow that runs away from his antagonists. So the contemporary enemy and peer pressure force the adrenal syndrome into antiquity.

A person that understands this syndrome can use it to great advantage if you use it as an attacking tool, especially against an enemy that doesn't understand it. As I said we are manipulating man's natural instinct to want to run as opposed to fight. By triggering adrenaline in an opponent I am also triggering his flight response. When he feels like running away, because society looks poorly on a 'runner', it will cause the opponent massive self-doubt and, hopefully cause him to capitulate. Everything in life has its opposite and the danger with any positive adrenaline switch is that it can backfire on you. If the recipient overrides the urge to capitulate the release may make him stronger and faster – a dangerous adversary indeed. I only use a positive adrenaline switch if I see a chink in the opponent's armour. This perception has come from many years of dealing with violence and violent people. If you can' t read an opponent then I wouldn't recommend employing this tactic, better to stick with submissiveness and use it as a negative adrenaline switch.

I remember hearing a great story about one of the old Japanese Sensie, Master Abbe, a world renowned martial arts teacher. He was walking down a quiet suburban street on his way home after his usual, evening teaching session. He noticed three youths hovering, several yards away on the opposite side of the street. When they approached him he was ready. 'Give us your money, or you'll get hurt,' said the leader of the three. Master Abbe looked at each one in turn, then casually took his wallet out of his jacket pocket, throwing it on the floor between himself and his antagonists. He pointed to the wallet and said, 'I' m prepared to die for that wallet. What about you?' The three would-be attackers looked at the wallet on the floor, then at Abbe, then at each other. Without further ado they all ran away, obviously not prepared to die for the wallet. Master Abbe picked up his wallet and calmly walked home.

I have used this type of approach dozens of time successfully myself. However, there is a danger with posturing: if it doesn't work and the assailant overrides his natural instinct to run/ freeze then you could be in trouble. You have certainly lost the element of surprise that's for sure. If you throw a challenge it may be met and accepted. If it is you had better be able to back it up or be able to back pedal in a hurry. I never throw a challenge unless I am totally committed to following that challenge through should it be accepted. It is fair to say that if you don't believe in what you are saying then your potential assailant won't believe you either. If he thinks that you are blagging him, he won't be psyched out. Personally I train in match fighting as a part of the back up, support system so that I am ready to take that challenge should it be accepted. Many people do not and are completely flummoxed when their antagonist says, 'Yeah, okay, I'll have some of that!' This causes an adrenal rush in you and the whole process is reversed. So, if this approach is employed be committed to follow it through – just in case.

A friend of mine tried the veteran approach. He told his antagonist in a very calm manner that if he wasn't happy that they would have to 'Sort it out on the common', not really expecting him to meet the challenge. 'All right,' came the reply, 'let' s do it now!' My mate dropped his bottle quicker than a greasy palmed milkman. The bottom line was, he had no idea of how to do a 'square go' (a match fight)

I often teach people, as a pre-cursory action trigger to pre-emptiveness, to ask their assailants a question to engage their brain. The question can be relative to what is happening or abstract, 'Is your mum's name Elsie?' or 'How's your mother/family/brother, these days?' Many of my students have found this effective. An excellent by-product of this is, the potential attacker doesn't realise that it is an engaging ploy and often thinks his chosen victim has recognised him, and really does know his mother/brother/sister. Again they often beat a hasty retreat before attack. This kind of ploy is only useful in the very early stages of the attacker's ritual and only if the locale is right. If you have been abducted or are completely detached from the herd it could be dangerous. Many attackers kill their victims if they think that they have been recognised. In all these cases your intention is to frighten the adversary, via your portrayal, into bottling it. The common street term for this process is 'Psyching Out' .

Climbing inside the opponent and switching on/off his fight or flight reaction to beat him with guile, as opposed to force, is advanced play and needs a great understanding to employ with conviction. Practice is of the essence if you want it to work and not backfire on you. I go into greater detail on the subject in my autobiographical books about my ten years as a nightclub doorman *Watch My Back – A Bouncers Story*, *Bouncer* and *On The Door – Further Bouncer Adventures*.

Chapter Five

Restraint

Restraint is often talked about in the martial arts fraternity. Does it work? Doesn't it work? Many police instructors have made a career out of teaching restraining techniques. Personally I think the only kind of truly effective restraint is unconsciousness. Knock them out and they're restrained. The rest of the time any kind of restraining technique is at best dodgy. The only time I have found restraints effective is when the opponent lets me put the technique on (like they do in so many police training schools), or if I am facing a very weak opponent. The rest of the time it is just too risky. Someone that wants to fight properly will not be restrained. For those times when restraint might be an option we'll explore one or two techniques, after all it is a part of fighting without fighting.

Spin and choke

I have used this technique on a few occasions but only when I sensed the threat was not great or I had the element of surprise on my side. The spin and choke off the fence is a technique I used when I felt that a restraint was viable. Note: I never tried to restrain anyone that was a high risk threat, it would be too dangerous, only use this if the threat is low risk and you feel you can get away with it.

Restraint—
choose the method
that will work well
for YOU.

The illustrations show the 'spin an choke' much better than I can describe it here. Basically when I felt the threat was beyond dissuasion and escape I asked a question to engage the opponent's brain and sharply pushed his left shoulder with my right hand and pulled his right shoulder with my left hand, spinning him so that his back was to my chest. I then wrapped my right arm around his neck and coupled up with my left to make the choke. From here you have the option, and this will be determined to how he reacts, to talk him down using the choke as leverage to persuade him, or choke him out if he persists in being violent. If you are working in security you also have the option of dragging him off the premises using the choke.

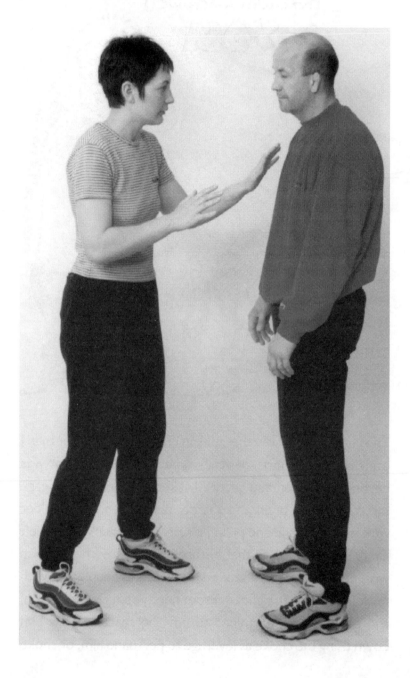

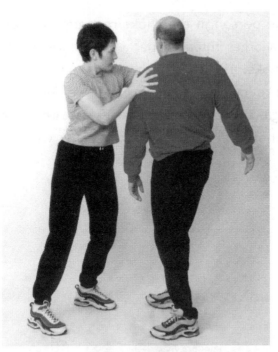

The Art of Fighting Without Fighting

If you have one person in the choke/restraint and are approached by another potential attacker, release your left hand from the choke, grip your shirt/top with your right hand to keep the choke 'on' and use the left hand as ' fence' to keep the other guy at bay. All the time being very careful not to leave the choke on too heavy or the guy will fall unconscious.

If the other attacker persists in coming forward re-connect the choke and turn the guy that you are choking towards his friend/accomplice so that he is now 'fence' between you and he. If the second attacker still persists and you think that an attack may be imminent (some people get very upset when you touch their mates), you may be forced to place the choke on full and KO the person that you are restraining. When you do so slam him onto his back, unconscious, between you and his friend. His KO' d body will act as fence between you and attacker number two. This will give you ample time to escape.

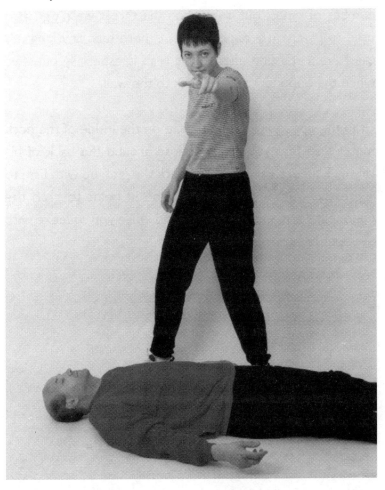

The Art of Fighting Without Fighting

Beware: this is a highly dangerous technique that should always be used with great care. Many have been choked to death, usually by accident, with this technique. Practice it in the controlled arena until you have the control to employ it in a tempered manner. Of course there are more ways to choke or restrain off the fence, this is just an appetiser to give you direction should you prefer to restrain as opposed to attack.

Larynx grab restraint

Again only if the threat is minimal. I did use this technique a number of times, but only when the threat wasn't great. I used to psyche my opponents out more than anything – it can have a startling effect. This grab is especially effective when the opponent has his back to the wall.

Grab the opponent by the throat, on the inside of the neck muscles so that your fingers close around the back of his larynx. Squeeze very hard and back the grab up with firm to aggressive verbal commands. It often helps to grab the opponent's arm with your left hand while you squeeze with the right hand.

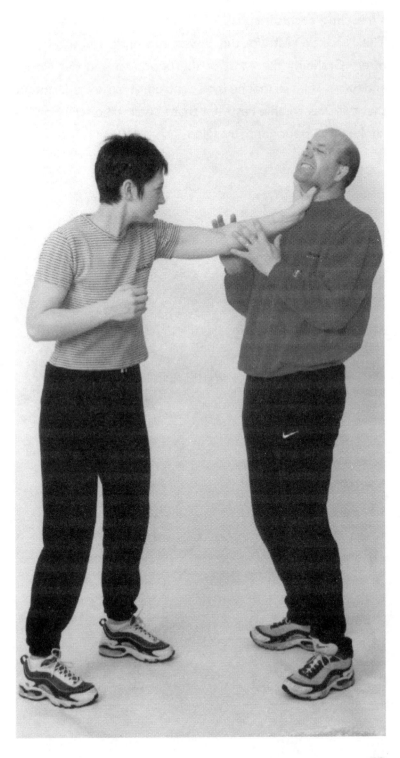

Wrestling restraint

This is a little restraint that Awesome Anderson used very often. Grabbing the wrist of the opponent and the elbow and turning him so that he is off centred, as illustrated. I found that this was an able restraint that I could take straight to a choke if the opponent struggled.

The Art of Fighting Without Fighting

Double wrist restraint

This was a useful restraint to use if the opponent had anything in his hand, like a glass or a bottle. Grab both wrists and hold them tightly to his sides. Be very careful though of the threat from head butting.

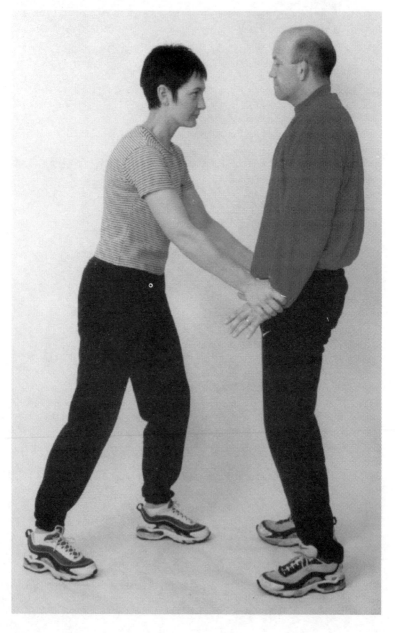

If you need to attack from here you can head butt the opponent

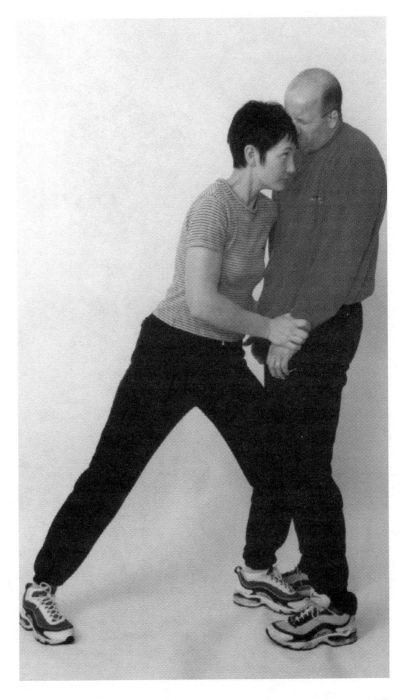

or take him in a wrestler bear hug – literally picking him up and throwing him to the floor or carrying him out.

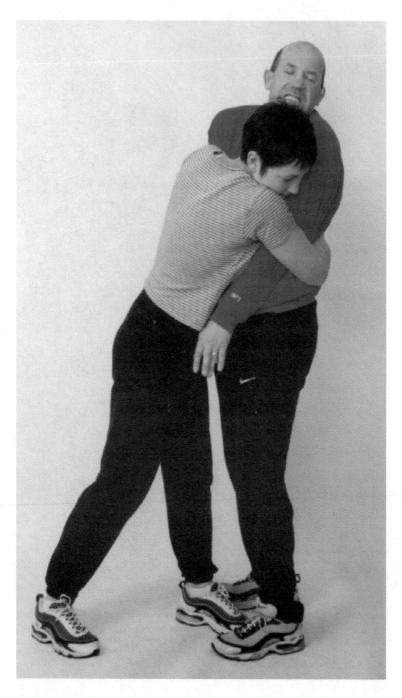

Unfortunately that is about the extent of my restraining techniques, or at least the ones that I think might have any chance of working. I know millions more that I could show you, but they are ineffective, so I'd rather not bother if you don't mind. I'm sure that there are people who have found other half desent restraints and if they work that's great, use them if you think they'll work for you. Always be wary of them though. The prison service teaches a lot of restraints, but they are all two and three (or more) men restraints that will not work for one on one.

What I would also say is, if you are facing more than one man, attempting restraint is suicide. When your hands are tied up trying to restrain one man and his mate/s are kicking your head in. or worse still sticking a knife in you. It is potentially fatal when dealing with more than one opponent anyway, to try and restrain them would be foolhardy.

Conclusion

This is a book about the art of fighting without fighting, so I have done my utmost to keep any kind of offensive strategies out of it. I did consider doing a chapter on the pre-emptive attack, should all else fail, but that does not constitute 'fighting without fighting . So what I would rather do is refer you to any of the other books I have written on the art of 'having a fight', specifically *The Three Second Fighter*, which concentrates on attacking off the fence.

The Last Resort. (see 'The 3 second fighter" for more detailed instructions.)

This book is not comprehensive neither are the concepts cast in stone; there are some ingenious ways of avoiding fights that others might be able to teach you. The techniques herein may also be tailored to fit you as a person. I think that avoiding violent conflict is definitely the way forward if we are to grow as a spiritual species. Not everyone agrees with me, but the world would be a pretty dull place if we all thought the same. For those that disagree, I respect your opinion. For those reading this book who are not sure who to listen to, I say go with your heart. If that isn't clear then look at the background of those offering advice. If you had two men trying to give you advice about swimming who would you listen to, the one swimming lengths of the pool in the deep end or the one with the rubber ring around his waist in the shallow end? I rest my case.

Good luck with your training, love and respect to you all and God bless to those with some means of invisible support. Above all, be a nice person and karma will be kind to you.

Geoff Thompson
1998.